The Gray In Me

A treasury of reflective poems

Sharmil Nanjappa

BookLeaf Publishing

India | USA | UK

Made with ♥ on the BookLeaf Publishing Platform
www.bookleafpub.in
www.bookleafpub.com

Dedication

For every story and every dream
For every cry and every beam
Through everything that time has seen
and for the magic that has been,

to my twin sister, Sheetal.

Preface

The poems in this book explore the darker emotions that lie within us. The first two poems dwell on the cycle of life and death, from a panoramic view. They reflect the insignificant life we choose to lead, unaware of our true self.

The collection is divided into three,

Part One: A reflection of one's lesser acknowledged emotions.

Part Two: A reflection of the grayer tones of life through nature.

Part Three: A reminder to accept and own the gray within, because one's strength lies in finding and understanding oneself.

Acknowledgements

I was a boat without an oar,
it was family who guided me towards the shore.
Adjusting sails with a friend or two,
when the winds wouldn't let me through.

I wade forward, don't stop my swim
even when the waters look grim,
Holding on to your strength and standing tall,
for what would I be without you all.

Green with Gray

A life that once danced with the winds
Lays buried with its sorrows and sins,

Wet and cold it had to surrender
Left with just a memory to remember.

A gray tombstone stands tall
The touch of fresh grass whispers it all,

Love and life of a heart that once stirred
All that green, makes death look undeserved.

A patch of green right next to gray,
just like a blip of life right next to death.

Blip

A drop of dew
A grain in the brew
A thorn in the weeds
A note lost amongst the beats

Hustling every second in time
Yet nothing that I can call mine,
Every moment when I get a grip
Reminds me, that I am just a blip.

Part One

Shame

A broken vase, a broken dream
A broke heart, a broken me.

It's your fault! I hear the blame
Can't you ever get it right? The voices are hard to tame
I need to own up for my mistake
But my failures would label me a fake,
O look, the great know it all,
Tripped on her toes and had a fall.
The sniggers, the whispers, all so loud
Inside my head, they all crowd.

I do not want to own up
I do not know how to shut them out,
I cannot find the strength to live up to my name
This shame of being broken, will never let me be the
same.

Fear

Would you trust my eyes? Even when they lie,
Stay by my side? Even when I snide,

When the lights go out, and I sit still
Would you sit beside, in the darkened chill?

Would you still smile, with your punctured pride?
Would you walk these miles with an ugly bride?

When my dried leaves fall, would you pick them all?
Or would you rather, follow a flower's call?

Anger

I am not the fiddle of your plans
Nor do you hold my threads in your hands
You can't beat me on my own board
I am not that meed for you to hoard.

Close my eyes and pray in defiance
I pray for your grief
I pray for your fall
I pray you never have it all.

I pray for your greed
may it grow more than your needs.
I pray that you bleed
befitting for your every single deed.

Pride

Is this all I have ? I need more.
For all that I am, my measure should show more.

Can't allow a single spec of dirt
Until the balance tips off
Too little, no this isn't my worth
My crown should weigh more than a collar's scoff

So, you peddle and you struggle
every drowning phase, going through the same cycle.

For pride
again, takes you for a ride,
It won't let you rest, won't let you be
Will never allow you to settle, don't you see?

Resigned

I can smile like her, sure I can.
Need to be like her, sure I will.

Stroke his ego
Soft as a doe
I can play nice
Not be the difficult type
Let him have the final say
Follow the crumbs at the end of day,

She is the one he approves of, she is the one he loves

It will get better once I behave like her.
Not myself, but her.

Pity

I carried everyone's pain
Held their tears, though there was nothing to gain
Covered their mistakes, took their fall
Knowing that I would lose it all.

I was good, I was kind
Letting it all slide behind,

My unsaid words now churn inside
My loathed cries have nowhere to hide
For them, every part of me died
and they left me with nothing, only their lies.

Part Two

Moon

Beautiful!
I see it up in the sky
How I wish I could touch its shine.

Speckles of clouds come by
Feels amiss without the moon in sight

The roads dry out but a puddle remains
In it I see a crescent white stain
So close, so bright,
How I wish I could touch its shine.

I plunge my hand forward and
Splash! I see the ripple

Oh dear!
What a fool I was to think I could touch a piece of you.

Rain

Watch the lands fondly greet
the dancing rains that fall deep,
Lost in an energetic beat,
Setting them all free.

In new hope every corner is drenched,
grateful as its thirst is quenched.
The same place in motion,
Yet somehow a very different one.

What an illusion the rains are bringing in
blurring the rigid reasoning that lies within!

Wildflower

A sun-kissed colorful spread
Across the dried mountain ahead
Made you strain your neck
Gave you a moment of bliss you would never forget.

Is that who I am?

Loved only on the best days of my dance
But left aside without a glance
on the days I have no bloom
leaving me all alone with my gloom.

This too, is who I am.
The dried days are still me.
Every new wrinkle is still me.

Buoy

The weather is rough
Yet the ship inches ahead with trust.
The buoy will never sink me to the floors
It will take me home to the shores.

On troubled waters the buoy will remain
For it is bound by its name
Silent and stifled by its pain
For it is one that must be chained.

Waves

Sandcastles and scribbled names
Laughter and floating frames
In a second all wiped off by the waves.

For every clean slate the tide brings in
For every receding memoir's din
The un-thanked waves rush and shout
'These shores will be indebted to me throughout.'

Sunset

I watch with tiny specks of sand on my shoes
The golden ball leaving colorful hues,

With every passing minute in time
The sun sets and with it so does my prime.

Part Three

Apart

You were a canvas waiting to be sprayed
But they always had to have a say,
And you could never find yourself free
Because they just wouldn't let you be.

On new palettes, mixing a little bit of each
But togetherness was just beyond reach.

Because they want red and you are white
Both best when kept on opposite sides.

Heart

Oh, they all walk in through the door
and they all bring with them hope.

Teach me to love, fill me with dreams
About a life beyond imaginations seams

But in the end, they have done their time
Leaving me with this empty silence of mine.

Yet, I seem to have all that I need
Everything is how it is meant to be,
It is just me, with me,
All me.

Repeat

Every day brings in a new wave
and I find myself move a mile ahead

Every day brings back an unpleasant memory
and I seem to go back a century

Back and forth
Trailing off course,
Front to back
Never on track,

And in this cycle that they call life
I seem to find,

Just about an hour to gauge my reality
Spared with just a minute to breath
And within it, less than a second to find me.

Trap

There is only one enemy
Who else but your own self,

Silently seeping from within
Keeping a record of your every sin,
There is no excuse, no escape.

How long can you run?
How long can you hide
but from your own mind?

Master

No smile
No pretend
No words, no sugarcoat

Let it ache, let it pain
This darkness is still you.

Hold it close
On your sleeve
It is one that will never leave

Draw the line,
Tame your child

The master is still you
The power is still you,
Only you.

More

A tiny drop
from the downpour,
Falls through the winds
Soothing it some more

Touches the green
A withering leaf's last seen
Onto a pebble on the ground
A heartbeat of a sound
Seeping further down
Quenching the knots underground.

One tiny drop, never knew what laid ahead
All it did was, be.
One tiny you, stuck between things, instead
All you need is to let yourself be.

Within

Not the medals on the wall
Not the times that you fall
Not about the detours you take
Not about the mistakes you make,

As small as you are
Like a falling star
This journey is yours to take.

Within, go deep inside
Search for the wounds that hide
Listen to belief on your side
Stay, let the silence guide.

Take this journey and find you.